MW00720574

COFFEE TALK

BY DONNA LAGORIO MONTGOMERY

ST. JOHN'S PUBLISHING

6824 OAKLAWN AVENUE, EDINA, MINNESOTA 55435

COFFEE TALK

A St. John's Book / Spring 1995

Cover art and illustrations by Laurie Montgomery

Published by
St. John's Publishing, Inc.,
6824 Oaklawn Avenue, Edina, Minnesota, 55435.

ISBN 0-938577-09-3

PRINTED AND BOUND IN THE UNITED STATES OF AMERICA
First Edition.
0 9 8 7 6 5 4 3 2 1

To Donna:
(my namesake!)
Let's talk!
Donna Montgomery

CONTENTS

COFFEE TALK

Coffee talk
is women's way
of counseling
each other.
"Your kid
did that?
It's no surprise,
mine did it
years ago."

In early years
each marriage
always seemed
so perfectly flawless;
it's comforting
to discover
dissatisfaction's
not uncommon.
The gossip mill
goes strong
from early years
'til later.

But if someone
really hurts
support is
right there
when it's needed.

Eventually,
PTA and church talk
give way to
that of perfect grandchildren
unlike any others,
plans for retirement,
bladder problems,
and physical degeneration
in general.

Talk of future plans
defers to
happy reminiscing
of the past,
while old problems,
retold,
generate laughter
instead of tears.

Coffee talk:
women sharing,
taking turns at listening.
No problem solving
needs to happen,
just being there
at full attention
to cheerlead
for each other.

WOMEN

Let's celebrate together,
my friend,
while there's still time.
I want to hear what
you've been up to
and tell you about me.
Let's walk, and talk
about nothing in particular:
our families,
friends, and dreams.
We'll have a cup of coffee
later,
and use our precious time
together
to relish our womanhood,
remember our childhood,
laugh, and cry.

Years fly by;
days that were so harried
in our early years
give us time now to reflect,
remember.

We need to do that together
as only women can.
Golden years are here,
our children living
testimony to us.
We have the right
to celebrate
our job well done.

Faithful friend,
heart of my heart,
tell me,
has life been good to you?

Before death traps us
unwanted,
when we're in our prime
with so much left to do,
let's celebrate together,
my friend,
while there's still time.

BIRTH DAY

Not too many years ago
the world was missing
a very important person.
Life in a certain house
was less exciting
and certainly
much more
predictable.
This same house was
minus the clutter
of projects completed
and others
never to be finished.
The sounds of a child's
laughter and tears
or shouts and whispers
were yet to be heard
through your voice.

15

And the special talents
you bring to family
and friends,
neighborhood
and community,
were not a part
of anyone's world.
I can't imagine
life for any of us
without you.
You make a difference!
So celebrate
your birth
with all of us,
and remember
what a special
present you are
for so many people.
Happy Birthday!

MOTHERHOOD

Motherhood is a condition
acquired most of the time
with no previous
knowledge,
education,
training, or desire.

And yet, it's the most
important, difficult, rewarding,
depressing, and exhilarating job
a woman can have.

The feeling when a newborn
is placed in mother's arms
will always be remembered.
Responsibility takes on
new meaning,
changing life for everyone
forever.

From beautiful, innocent,
toddling twos,
to emotional,
hair-trigger teens,

life becomes a rollercoaster
of peaks and valleys.

Busy moms sometimes forget
to enjoy each new phase
of their child's development;
there's so much left to do
at the end of the day.

Daily work never
comes to an end.
Wash three loads of laundry;
miss a day and do six.
Prepare three meals in between,
clean house, scrub and bake.

Nurturing children is the goal,
but sometimes in the hurry
of meeting physical needs,
emotional needs of everyone
are neglected.

So when the time comes
for accounting to another,
blessings on you
magician mother.
May yours be the golden chariot
in the carpool to heaven.

FATHERHOOD

The job description
for fatherhood
has evolved
and expanded
over time,
from family provider
and observer
to active participant.

Today, dad can be found
changing diapers,
cooking dinner,
cleaning house,
driving carpools,
taking kids on outings,
or doing laundry.

Mom and dad
are equal partners
in family fun
and responsibility,
making them closer
in their love,
and therefore,
better parents.

Dad is now allowed
to show tender emotions
that somehow
add to his strength
rather than
diminish it.

The world has been
unrelenting and dictatorial
about the fatherhood role,
but times have changed.
Dad is now allowed
to show his heart,
making everyone winners.

BABY

Ho, hum,
dum-de-dum.
I'm bored,
suck my thumb.

Wet my pants,
cry for mom,
here she comes,
dum-de-dum.

Now I'm hungry,
what's to eat?
Cry for mom,
here's a treat.

What a racket,
get my jacket,
in the car,
lulled to sleep.

Why grow up?
I've got it made.
(Put my stroller
in the shade!)

Ho, hum,
grunt and point;
no need to talk,
what a joint!

LITTLE GIRLS

Little girls are supposed to
be made of
sugar and spice
and everything nice . . .
and they are . . .
but that's just the
beginning.

Baseball games
and shopping sprees,
quiet walks
among the trees,
noisy parties, overnights,
next door neighbor
quickie fights.
Growing up
will not be easy,
eating chocolate
'til you're queasy.

What will you decide to do?
You can now be
anything you choose.
Space scientist,
doctor,

engineer,
are but a few choices
for your career.
Right now
you have so many voices,
I'm sure great grandma
(wherever she is)
rejoices.

So take your time
and think it out.
There's just one job
unique to you.
Motherhood,
all husbands note,
will never be
their option . . .
nope.

LITTLE BOYS

Little boys are supposed to
be made of
snips and snails
and puppy dog's tails . . .
and they are . . .
but that's just the beginning.

Sports and games,
giving gifts,
reading poetry,
healing rifts,
enjoying nature
in all its beauty,
not just because you
feel a duty.
Don't be afraid
to feel emotion;
reward will be
your wife's devotion.

Beginning now,
my little boy,
a doll may be
your favorite toy.
Or baseball bats
and motor cars,
the choice is yours,
shoot for the stars.

Just be the best that
you can be;
that's good enough for
you and me.
And remember, dear,
the greatest part . . .
you're now allowed
to show your heart.

ONCE UPON A TIME

Once upon
a time,
long ago
and far away,
I remember
every single
fairy tale
cliche.

Before tucking
kids in bed
and kissing them
at nighttime,
gently read
a tender poem:

29

a nightmare
nursery rhyme.
Losing kids
deep in the forest,
poisoned apples,
spinning wheels,
kissing girls
until they cry,
wolves at houses
(. . . how do you feel?)

Each was filled
with murder,
perversion,
or assertion.
Happy childhood
memories
of cruel stepmothers
and desertion.

Sleep well,
sweet dreams
my child; let me
hear your laughter,
because somewhere,
I remember,
they lived
happily ever after.

ARE WE ALMOST THERE?

"Are we almost there?"
my youngster asks
as our trip's
about to start.
It's the first
of many times
the listless question
will be asked.

Down the road,
out to the highway,
about to start
ten hours of driving,
comes the question
once again,

"Are we almost there?
How much farther?"

Enjoy the scenery,
watch the cows,
see the horses
in pastures green.
What a sight
is here around us,
hours of peace
to contemplate.

"Are we almost there?
How much longer?"
as we approach
hour number two.
Only eight more
left to travel,
"are we almost there"
is getting old.

Halfway through
our well-planned journey,
questioning child
falls asleep.
Thank you Lord
for little blessings
that you toss our way
each day.

Ten hours later,
tummys rumbling
from McDonalds
along the way,
we arrive
in good condition.
"Yes, little youngster,
we're finally here!

FIRST CHILD

Good morning, new world!
Yesterday morning
I woke up a woman;
this morning
I woke up a mother.
What miracle has happened
to me?

My husband and I
have been in
partnership with
God
in the creation of life.
You breathe.
You live.

My precious child,
I pledge I'll
honor and love you
unconditionally always.
You're so
helpless now,
you can't even
roll over without help.

I 'll serve your
every need,
never being too busy
to hear what you're saying
or to take time to
examine the tiniest flower
on the tiniest weed
with you.

And when the time comes,
I will gently
encourage you to become
independent to the
degree you're able.
Until then,
my precious gift, may I never
intentionally
hurt your tender heart.

MIDDLE CHILD

What luck!
All the experimenting
was done
on number one child.
Now all the fussing
is driving
the youngest one wild!
No wonder I'm so
cool and laid back.
If I play my cards right
I can get lost in
middleness
and avoid
accountability.

Don't rock the boat
is my operating theme.
Keep the waters still
and slip by quietly,
causing no waves
of recognition that might
put ideas of work
done or undone
into parents' thoughts.

I love being middle.
My parents are
broken in properly now,
making up
for previous mistakes
made on others
by being extremely careful
about condemning any
questionable behavior of mine.
I hope their guilt
keeps active
until I leave home.

So thank you oldest sibling.
Thank you younger ones, too,
for taking on all that
responsibility
so I can relax and enjoy
the perks
of being a carefree,
happy-go-lucky
middle child.
What luck!

LAST CHILD

Where do I begin
my thoughts about you,
baby of our family?
We've had so much
fun together,
being friends
as well as family.

Somehow, circumstances
seemed to dictate
a different relationship
with you.
The whole family
felt it.
Besides us,
your regular parents,
all the children took you
lovingly under their wings
and we were all
parenting partners.
Instead of becoming spoiled
with all the attention,
you responded
with unselfconscious love

in return,
much more than we could ever
anticipate and expect.
Your enthusiasm is
contagious.
Whether we watch
a beautiful sunset
together
or share an ice cream cone,
you couldn't be more
appreciative,
never failing
to thank your benefactor
abundantly and sincerely.

Sweetness manifests itself
in your beautiful,
spontaneous smile.
What a happy heart
you are,
making life so fun
for all of us.
You've taught us
about a deeper kind of
unquestioning love.
Thank you for being
just the way you are.

ATTENTION: MOM TO CHILD

Katie, Laurie, Amy, MOLLY,
can you give me a hand?

Yes, mom,
but after
all these years,
why can't you
remember my name,
since I'm
the only child
left at home?

Of course I can
Tim, Joan, Patrick, MOLLY.
(There I go again!)
I don't know why
everyone else's name
is always on
the tip of my tongue.
No matter whom I want,
the family litany
is first recited.
Sometimes relatives
I haven't seen for years,

or neighbors
from another decade,
appear mysteriously
in the countdown;
I have no prejudice.
When listening
to my friends talk
to their children,
I discover
the illness is common
to all mothers,
no matter our age
or physical condition.
So I guess
it simply comes
with motherhood.
Isn't that right,
Mike, Johnny, Tony, MOLLY?

SMELLING THE ROSES

We're in the middle
of a most exciting universe.
We should take time
to carefully observe it
so we can teach our children
to be good observers.
Year after year nature's seasons
unfold their splendor before us,
but we seem to miss the beauty
of their comings and goings.

The order and consistency
in nature should never cease
to amaze us.
The tiniest flower
on the tiniest weed
is consistent always.
Robins come back in the spring.
Buds appear at the
same time each year.

The sun rises every morning
in the east
and sets every night
in the west.

We can smell rain in the air,
grass freshly cut,
lilacs in bloom,
or a field of alfalfa.

Isn't it amazing that with
millions of cells in our bodies
they all end up in the
right place at birth?
Isn't it a wonder that
cats have hair,
cows have hides,
turtles have shells,
fish have scales,
animals have instincts,
and we have minds?
Think of it!
Think of everything
you can see in nature
and be awed by it.
Then teach your children
to be awed by it.

THE FAMILY REFRIGERATOR

If refrigerators
could talk,
they'd certainly
have a lot
to share.
Silent guardians
of a family's
personal history:

appointments of the week,
PTA and church news,
luncheons and recitals,
an indoor billboard
for children's
art projects
from earliest efforts.

Sports carpools
and family schedules,
as well as
daily chore charts,
make them
the center of attention
and gathering spot
for major family briefings.
The clutter
and disarray
of postings
on their surfaces
are testimony
to a constantly changing
but vital family organizer role.

Later, when the
family's gone,
in their maturity,
though tape marked
and battle weary,
our refrigerators
become more dignified
in their finery.
More than likely,
photos are now placed
neatly in organized rows,
gathering info on the
scattered families,
reminding moms and dads
to hold fast
in their hearts
so many precious memories
of earlier years,
because refrigerator historians
chronicled it all.

MY KITCHEN WINDOW

My kitchen curtain
rises daily
on the neighborhood theater;
time is
of no consequence.
The play is on
at my convenience,
sunrise to sunset.

Ribbons of children
unwind down the street,
meeting others of all
shapes, sizes, and colors
at the bus stop,
or simply gathering
in colorful bows
winding up to
their school.

Next the
parade of parents
walking to buses
or driving
frosty cars
to jobs they love or hate,

49

never questioning
their need to go.

After school,
and summer,
the plot improves:
intrigue, comedy,
suspense,
sorrow,
as children interact
with each other
in ways
they learned at home.

Enjoy your youth
dear children,
for soon enough
you'll be the audience
at the kitchen window.

FAMILY TRINITY

Wise people for centuries
have debated
a mystery of faith:
the Trinity,
three persons
in one,
Father,
Son,
and Holy Spirit.
How can
three be one,
yet each separate?

Then we marry
and have a family.
No longer is there
any mystery.
In fact, the Trinity
becomes extremely easy
to understand.

When man and woman
marry
they become one
but still maintain
their individuality.
The family trinity
becomes complete
when a child is born:
the third person
of the trinity
and definitely the spirit.

Three persons in one.
How quickly the
mysterious Trinity
becomes understandable
and simplicity itself.

HAPPY ANNIVERSARY

We begin a new year
with each other.
I wake up and see
your familiar face
across the pillow
and know all is
right with the world.

How different we are
than when we were
courting.
We wouldn't recognize
each other
from pre-marriage days.

Growing into life together
brings our love
full circle, sometimes daily.

Love started
as a small blossom
on a tree,
opened full bloom
during courtship,
then grew into
unripe fruit:
at first too hard and in
need of time to mature
and soften.
With the sweetness
of maturity came fruit
ripe for enjoyment
and bountiful in numbers.

I love you still,
but now it's
more comfortable
and habitual.
We know each other's
thoughts and dreams.

They can be spoken
or unspoken.
Reality and wisdom
temper our relationship.

I can't imagine
living without you
or our family
to whom we have given life.
I'd do it
all over again,
knowing all
I know now.
Happy Anniversary.

MY HUSBAND

Our dreams of yesterday
are changing, my husband.
How have we done?

Wealth has eluded us,
at least material wealth
connected with fame.
Wealth comes, instead,
from our children.

The house we thought
would long since be paid for
has a second mortgage.

No savings are in the bank,
but our children are educated
and supportive in many ways.

Our own relationship
has had its peaks and valleys,
. . . ah, yes, its peaks and valleys.
Did we spend too much time
with children
and not enough with each other?

57

My service role is changing.
I, always wife and mother,
never thinking of nor fulfilling
my own needs,
have discovered me, myself,
my own person
with self worth of my own.
It's exciting. It's scary.
It's exhilarating.

What happened to
yesterday's dreams,
my husband?
Those dreams are changing.
Yes.

Yesterday's dreams are changing,
and all that has happened
hasn't been able
to break our spirits.

The lace and fluff
of our wedding day
have taken new form.
We're muslin and denim:
mended, remended and patched.

Our dreams have changed,
my husband.
How have we done?

. . . tell me,
 and I'll tell you.

DAD

I remember fondly
many hours shared
standing beside
my dad's workbench
doing busy work
while he
repaired something broken,
whistling a sweet melody
while deep
in his own thoughts.

He was a quiet, patient man,
so respected and loved
by his children
that we would never
do anything
to cause him sorrow.
To disappoint him
would be more
than we could bear.
And so, by his example,
we learned of gentle love
and tender hearts.

In all my years,
he never had to
pound a lesson into me
by spanking,
and I'll always remember
his last
tender words to me,
because they were
about me.
In my middle years,
when wrinkles were
quite evident,
as well as extra pounds,
he looked at me
with loving eyes
and told me,
"You're beautiful, kid,
inside and out."
What beautiful words
to be his last legacy . . .
my self-fulfilling prophecy.

GRANDMA

Now I'm as my mother's
mother:
a grandma . . .
rejoicing in seeing my
children's children grow.

Grandchildren,
what fun you are!
My job is changing;
no more am I responsible
for the all consuming
care-giver job of my youth.

I'm a conspirator
in your secret child's world.
I plan and plot
excursions and lunches,
or safaris into imaginary places,
through tall tales and

beautiful books.

I've grown to realize
I can't solve all your
problems,
but instead, can patiently listen
while you learn
from the telling,
then solve them
yourself.

I'm privileged to
pass through your world for
whatever time I'm allowed,
taking all I've learned
in foresight
and using it well
in hindsight
to guide and entertain you.

When it comes
that I must leave you,
remember me for
all the good times,
and know that I go
with anticipation
to see new worlds,
and begin
my next adventure.

GRANDPA

Grandpas are special people
who never tell grandchildren
what they have to do
right now.
In fact, it can
usually wait until later,
after grandpa's stories
or after we play
another game of cards.
(It's harder to win at
playing cards with
grandpa than when
I play with grandma.)

We go for walks together
and he tells me
what he used to do
when he was my age,
and he tells me
what my parents did
at my age.
(I especially like it when
he tells me the naughty things
my parents did).
When we go

fishing together
grandpa makes me
bait my own hook.
I hate that part,
but he says that's what
good fishermen do.
And I watch grandpa
hold his pole real still
and close to the water
and try to do it
the same way.
But then I forget,
and eventually my line
gets all tangled up,
and Grandpa sits
patiently
and fixes it.

I love Grandpa so much.
When I grow up
that's what I want to be:
a grandpa.

CHILDREN JUST FIT

Isn't it amazing
the way mother's body
is made to serve her child?
How perfectly she's designed to
do all the things
she needs to do.
In view of the
remarkable intelligence
reflected in nature's designs,
is it really possible
we could have
just happened to exist?

Mother's arms bend
at just the right spot

for holding baby,
while fingers and hands
help with care.
Her breasts
are in the best place
to nurse baby
with her own milk
that mysteriously comes
only when needed.
Mother's knees bend
to reach her child's level,
while loving arms
enclose the tot or teen.
Mother's hands serve
to wash children and clothes,
prepare meals, give first aid,
pick up after everyone,
clean the house, make beds,
prepare treats,
and comfort the sick.

The miracle of the
human body
is a gift to everyone.
Children should be taught
to appreciate it
and use it wisely.

My Children

My dear little children
where have you gone?
I see you in hindsight as
sweet innocence and
laughter,
mischief rolled into
ring around the rosies and
downright joy.

I see myself walking with you
around the dining room table
in pre-dawn hours,
counting the minutes until the
doctor comes in his office
so we can visit him and
give you comfort.

You toddled so elegantly
into pre-teen years,

only to stumble
on low self-esteem
while you tried out
your newly developing body
in all its
awkward
self-consciousness.
Then your first love,
and with it
the beginning of your
new person.
From caterpillar to
butterfly
overnight.

I cried with you.
I laughed with you.
I will always love you
unconditionally.

My dear little children
I know where you've gone.
The circle is closing.
It's your turn to
watch
your dear little children
discover all that you know
. . . and more.

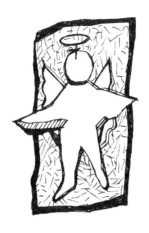

FAVORITE CHILD

(Don't tell the others,
but you're my
favorite child.)
I love the way
your enthusiasm for life
bubbles over into
everything you do,
first child.

(Don't tell the others,
but you're my
favorite child.)
You're such an athlete.
We're really proud of
the way you
train to win,
second child.

(Don't tell the others,
but you're my
favorite child.)
You've always been
so gentle,
we know you'll be a poet,
lovely, sensitive,
third child.

(Don't tell the others,
but you're my
favorite child.)
Full of joy and love,
you have taught us
so much,
baby of the family.

All right, favorite dad,
we're getting wise to you.
We plot and scheme
to trap you
to incriminate yourself
by admitting
who's your favorite
in front of all the others.
"So who's your favorite child?"
we ask diplomatic dad,
knowing well the answer
to that ancient,
oft asked leading question.
You don't really have to tell us
since we already know;
we're each your favorite child
and it always will be so.

LOSING A BEST FRIEND

Sadness is upon me;
my child broke
a trust today . . .
an honesty that was
between us
from her birth.
I never lied to her;
she never lied to me,
I thought,
because we were
not only mother and daughter
but best friends.

That has ended.
She set out
to purposely deceive me
and make me believe
that circumstances
were other than
they were.

There was no need
to lie to me.
This was not
the first time,
it appears,
when my protective eyes
were focused temporarily
in another direction,
that she became
another person.

What we once had
will never be again.
My best friend
has broken an unspoken,
irreparable trust
with a premeditated lie.
I know her choice
will be regretted
because our friendship
will never be
as it once was.
I lost my best friend today.
Life looks different.

Now its tomorrow,
and the hurt
is put in better perspective.
Things may never be the same,
but best friends
don't stop being best friends
because they've been
put to the test.
Best friends are forever.

MOTHERS NEED ENCOURAGEMENT

Motherhood is difficult.
Many are so discouraged
they just give up.
If a mother finds it necessary
to get a paying job
outside the home,
she's juggling two
very important careers.
Mothers who aren't employed
outside the home
are usually juggling
volunteer work.
It's not easy to be a mother,
and it's extremely difficult
to be a good one.

Mothers need support
and recognition.
Mothers are tough;
they've been through the fire.
They've lived through
kids loving them
and hating them,
good times and hard times.

Mothers know both
pride and humility,
acceptance and rejection.
No other group in the world
is so forgiving,
or been asked
to forgive so much,
over and over.

Mothers have mothers
of their own,
and now,
as mothers themselves,
possess a unique perspective.
Tell them almost anything,
they won't be shocked.
Reject them,
and they'll come back.
The worst thing would be to
ignore them.
Mothers, as much as anyone,
need encouragement.

MOTHER'S DAY

Once a year our nation
sets aside a special day
to honor mothers.
Florists and candy stores,
restaurants and
ice cream shops,
love mom
for many reasons
other than her
job description.

Small children scurry home
from school
with homemade treasures
clutched
(and sometimes crumpled)
in sweaty, grimy little hands.
Older kids say things
through cards and gifts
they never say
at other times of the year.

Dad occasionally
becomes a banker
and loan officer
to finance
mom's special day.

But, alas, there's
one fly in the ointment
of Mother's Day bliss:
who was the person,
the incredible child
not born of woman ,
who decided to have the
Fishing Opener
on Mother's Day?

LIFE WAS SIMPLE

When I was young,
life was simple.
Neighborhood kids
organized themselves
into teams
to play ball
or other games,
go on excursions
to the corner drug store,
or to Saturday matinees
with the group.
We gathered
around front steps
after school
and made our plans
for what
remained of each day
and early evening:
softball in the street
while daylight lasted,
and kick the can
at night under
corner street lights
that illuminated
our playing field.

Our neighborhood
was ethnic
in its composition
and also
in our hearts.
Catholics and "Publics,"
Christian and Jews,
our differences
didn't matter.
Our bonds
of neighborhood
transcended
all the mundane
social segregations
of the times.

We worked hard,
played hard,
and God help
any person
who tried
to fit us
into a tight,
confining mold.
Life really was simple
and carefree.

GETTING AWAY FROM IT ALL

There comes a time
when parents need a break
from their kids,
and quite true as well,
when kids need
a break from parents.

So let it be known,
dear children,
your parents are
running away from home.
We won't be gone long,
probably just for the weekend.

We have decided
not to stay too close,
like in this city,
because we'll be too easy
to find.
You'll want to visit
and use the hotel pool.

So here is our number.
We'll be one hundred miles
away.

We intend to talk,
and play,
and eat at a leisurely pace.

Maybe in the relaxed atmosphere
we'll even think of
something else
to do.

The bottom line is
time.
Time to speak to each other
without interruption,
be together without
the telephone ringing,
and enjoy a leisurely meal that
someone else has prepared for us,
served us,
and cleaned up after.
We won't even have to
make the bed
in the morning.

The extra bonus comes
when we return home
to find out we were
missed.
It's great to get away!

First Day of School

My little one takes
the first step
toward independence today.
(Are you frightened?
I am.)

Brand new crayons,
brand new shoes,
school bag briefcase
hiding show and tell.
(You seem so young
to begin a new career.)

Your hair is combed,
your hands are washed,
shoes are polished,
teeth are brushed.
(Does the teacher know
how dear you are?)

I wish you could be
small forever,
so I could hug you
and watch you grow.
But then I'd miss
the fun that's brewing
in all the years
of growth you'll know.

So step out confidently,
child.
The world's your gift
from us old timers.
Treat it well,
discover some secrets,
pass them on,
and watch them grow.
(Are you frightened?
No, just excited.)

JUNIOR HIGH

I'm so afraid
and so excited.
Will I measure up
or make a
fool of myself instead?
What if I do
something
to call attention
to myself?

I know I
forgot to do
something "major"
before I
caught the bus.
Is my hair
messed up?
Am I wearing
the right clothes?
More important,
please let me
look like
everyone else.
I'd die if
I were different.

Why can't I be
in my old school?
New bus,
new kids,
new driver;
I'll never get
used to this.

What if I forget
my locker combination
or come late
to class?
I'll never
survive this!

Hmm,
who's that
beautiful hunk
heading this way
and smiling at me?
New school,
new opportunities.
Oh. I just love
Junior High!

T-P'd

I woke up on
a snowless day
with no white
on the ground,
but trees were draped
in odd white strips,
with rolls of toilet paper
all around.

Mischievous gremlins
did their T-P dance,
noiselessly throwing
roll after roll.

Up again,
down again,
in tree after tree,
a crazy kind of popularity poll.

"Who did this mindless thing to us?"
I ask my silent children.
"This is an honor
bestowed on a few,"
they say, helplessly
suppressing a grin.

A phenomenon
of high school:
popular kids
will get T-P'd.
In the night,
like a thief,
classmates
do the white deed.

So party on,
friends of my child;
have your fun
on weekend nights,
but please, think of my kid
as an unpopular geek,
then pass our house
ever so quietly.

CURFEW

Curfew, curfew,
in the house,
I can slip in
like a mouse,
squirming under
a crack in the door,
while listening to parents
unworriedly snore.

My clothes are hidden
under a bush,
traded for pj's
to cover my tush.
Slip the car into neutral,
push it slowly down the street,
keeping lights turned off
'till my friends I greet.

Let my curfew be damned;
tonight I'll have fun,
my parents are oblivious
to what's being done.
Now back through the window
when evening is 'or,
no one is the wiser,
so I'll do it some more.

HIGH SCHOOL

At last,
I'm on my way
to adulthood.
Pretty soon
I'll be on my own.
Mom and Dad
always tell me,
"What's your hurry?"
I want to be
independent,
start college,
live on campus,
and meet new people.
I want to
grow up!

I hate
leaving my friends,
but we'll write,
and I'll make
many new friends.
It will be
so much fun to be
Independent!
For a few more years
I'll bide my time,
study well,
play hard,
and suck up.
Then I'm off!

Stood Up

I have a date
with the
grandest of men;
getting ready
I fret
like a mother hen.

I'm showered
and shined
with toenails painted;
if he doesn't
come soon
he'll see me fainted.

Where is that man
who promised
he'd be here?
Was somebody fibbing?
It's becoming quite clear.

Obsequious me
in my best
party dress,
is getting objective
through all
this distress.

The hour tells me
it seems
I'm stood up.
Assertiveness
now begins
helping this pup.

If he calls
in the morning
with any remorse,
I'll apologize profusely,
since I forgot our date
(. . . of course.)

SPRING BREAK

Hi-hi-dee-ho,
on Spring Break
I go!
Toss off the
snow shoes,
winter sweaters,
and quilted jackets.
On with the
sun-tan lotion and
three ounce
swim suit.
My mindworks evolve
from plodding labor
to light-hearted

99

fantasy.
My spirits are
as light as
my new
swim suit.

What I'll do
will never be shared.
It's my secret break
from reality.
But regrets there
will be none;
the week is
strictly for fun
and sun, sun, sun.
So think of me
now and again
as the north wind
blows over the land,
and know that
home or job or school
are words gone temporarily
from my vocabulary.
Hi-hi-dee-ho!

AWAY TO COLLEGE

Firsts are sometimes hard
as well as exciting.
Right before college
kids lose patience
with mom and dad
about so many things:
old-fashioned morals,
improper eating habits,
spare time unwisely spent,
and on and on.
They're feeling
intoxicated with freedom
from home, family,
and responsibility.

Enjoy, dear child,
because parent's time
is finally here.
We shed a tear
as life adjusts
to the new change,
but adjustment comes quickly.

After the first quarter ends
these same children
come home to visit,
and the stifling
four walls
which stunted their growth
now give
a warm welcome
and renew
old family memories.
Parents are hugged
in a very special way
and sought after for
their advice
and homemade cooking.

Wonder of wonders,
what a pity,
just when mom and dad
are having so much fun!

My Turn

I can't believe
the day has come.
Our last kid
started college.

Oh beautiful house!
We've seen so much,
we both deserve
a freshening touch.

The battlefield
is strangely quiet,
furniture urging me
to try it.

103

But first, let's
light the fireplace,
snuggle up with a book,
and relax with grace.

Deciding if I do so choose,
my special daily upper:
may very simply be today
popcorn with nothing else
for supper.

You have your freedom
with my blessing,
but I have mine,
I'll be confessing.

I've coveted
this special time,
when I have reached
my peak of time.

What fun to dance
and sing and shout,
no one to embarrass
or cause to pout.

Have fun at college,
child of mine;
I hope you always
will do fine.

Remember I'll think
of you a bunch
when I go out
with the girls for lunch.

The empty nest syndrome
is here at last.
(Who ever said
the years go fast?)

What went around
has come around;
it's mom's turn now,
my options abound!

BLOOMING

When I was
a little girl
(a few more years
than a short time ago)
I was obedient
and always did
as I was told.

In school
I listened to my teacher
. . . and always did
as I was told.

When in my teens,
I wanted only
to conform
and never make
the slightest wave
or call attention
to myself,
. . . so I did
as I was told.

During early marriage
and PTA years,
I conformed to the behavior
expected of good
wives and mothers,
. . . and I always did
as I was told.

But now responsibilities
are directed toward myself,
and wings that were
tightly compressed
against my sides
have opened
of their own accord
and refuse to be
put back into
their cocoon.
I flit and fly
from sun-up to dusk,
and trust me,
friend,
. . . I almost never do
as I am told.

College

I couldn't wait
to get here,
be independent,
be responsible,
and join the
swinging
generation.
My parents
were bugging me
and I had to
get away.
I'm an adult
and must be
about my business.

Finally
I'm studying
what I enjoy,
and will
soon decide
on my life's career.

But something
is bothering me
and I can't quite
put my finger
on it.
I think about home
a lot.
I wonder what
my family
is doing.
How are
the other kids?
I wonder if mom
has made my
favorite meal lately?
When's vacation?

Mom and Dad,
I know I'm
where I belong,
but I miss you all
so much.

GRADUATION

Yahoo!
This is it:
the end of one phase
of my education.
If I wasn't so ecology minded
I'd take all of my
books and papers,
run out to an open field,
and race around
the whole place,
letting the wind lift the papers
from my arms
to fly in a
white paper blizzard
while I throw each book
into the melee
like shooting stars
in the nighttime sky!

Am I happy?
I'm hysterical
and giddy
and free as a bird!

I'll dance all night long
and try to keep the joy
hostage in my soul,
rerunning the tape
at low times to
rejuvenate my body.

What's that you say?
Responsibility?
What do you mean?
Oh, now I'm an adult
with adult responsibility.
Right.
A job, career, apartment?
Oh, no! Is that
what this means?
But the job market
is depressed, and
apartments are so expensive
I'll have to share one
with two or three people.
Cook for myself?
But I haven't got enough time.

Adulthood? Responsibility?
Oh, to be young again!

GRADUATION DAY

We begin
our final journey
by car,
watching familiar scenery
pass by
for the last time.

The car is
as empty as
we can make it,
leaving room
for clothes,
furniture, bikes,
and memories
to be packed
and brought back
to their temporary home.

Our son or daughter
left a child
and returns
a young adult
with dreams
of wealth and riches,
a wonderful job,

and independence
painting beautiful
pictures in each head.

We anticipate
their moments in the sun,
as each graduate
walks slowly
across the stage,
alone,
to receive the degree
worked for so long.
  Such a brief moment
      for so many years
            of hard work.

Graduate.
You've earned
your day of glory.
Remember every
precious minute.
The day is yours.

Our trip home begins.
It's happy -
mixed with sad.
There were
so many tearful
goodbyes.

YOU TURNED OUT JUST FINE

Ah, hindsight!
If only parents
could have it
when dealing
in foresight!

In grade school
you were "disruptive,"
always wanting
to visit
at the wrong time.
(Today your
outgoing personality
is an asset.)

Then came
junior high
and a few calls
from the police
about groups
hanging around,
stoning street lights
or "cruising" on bikes
after I thought
you were tucked in
for the night.

You were tenacious,
though, with
part-time work,
sticking it out
with dubious
management
and no
encouragement
from supervisors.

Then costly college,
new found independence,
and live-in
arrangements
that caused me
many sleepless nights.

Where did the
years go?
Was the worrying
all for nothing?
Yes, absolutely yes,
because,
my dear child,
you turned out
just fine.

I TOLD YOU SO

I hate to say
"I told you so,"
but you know
that I did -
so many times
as you grew up,
you crazy
little kid.

Grade school art,
a great sports play,
sharing your treasures
with friend and foe,
you always were
the greatest kid,
and I'm happy that
"I told you so."

EMPTY NEST

The time has come
for me to be feeling
depressed and lonesome;
why aren't I?
What's wrong with me?

Strange feelings
are coming over me.
Feelings like
why aren't I anxious
or lonesome?
Why am I enjoying
my leisure so much?
Why is life so satisfying?

A large period of my life
is ending,
a time when
as it was
is no more.

My children have
left the nest,
leaving me alone
to meet myself
all over again.

What fun!
I love you
dear children
and look forward
to your visits,
and to those
of your children.
Please come often.
But please,
my dears,
don't move back.

THE VISIT

I feel like Christmas,
but it isn't.
Even better,
my child's
coming home
on vacation.

Will the house
look smaller?
Get it dusted,
bake favorite foods,
neglect unnecessary work,
and enjoy
anticipating a week off
to play and talk together.

So much
to catch up on;
you moved
so far away.
I'm proud of
your independence,
but I hate it, too.

Maybe that's because
I realize
the brevity of life.

You think
you'll live forever,
and so will I.
But that's
wishful thinking
on your part.
At my age,
I know the
swiftness of
a passing year
or decade,
and know we
pick up speed
on the downhill ride.

But for one whole week
we'll live
and expand to its utmost
every solitary minute
of each hour,
every day.

Then I'll store them
in my heart
to pull out
and relive
when you're gone.

If wishes
could come true
I'd tell you,
"Tap your heels,
believe and say,
'there's no place
like home,' "
then come to stay.

My Baby's In Love

My baby's in love
for the first time.
Be kind,
new love;
know that you're
in a position
to experience
a sweetness
and devotion
few ever know.

If this isn't
your first time,
please try to
go back
to when love was
new and beautiful
to you.
Treat my baby
gently,
appreciate her
tender heart,
and be kind.

If the time comes
when you decide
to move on,
do it with grace,
please,
and don't
cloud the air
with philosophizing
no one
cares about.

Leave as friends
with the same
kindness
you'd show a
stranger.
Please,
you won't have to
see the tears
her family will see.
Gently, gently,
please.

Engagement

Ring, ring, ring around my
finger,
my mind is obsessed
with my new ring!
I'll wear it always
and treasure its
promise of commitment
by both of us to each other.
My dear darling dearest
may life always be
as exciting and fun
and exhilarating as it is now,
right this moment, with you.

Our courtship had
its ups and downs,
preparing us for
the ups and downs of marriage.
Promise we won't
give up on each other,
but will work hard and
constantly to make our
life together permanent, yet fun,
unpredictable, and never boring.
Let's surprise each other
for no reason at all,
share a private dream, or
listen patiently to each other.

My husband-to-be,
I love to hear your voice
on the phone
or while sitting next to me
in the car, on a date, or
going shopping with you.

It doesn't matter what we do;
being quiet together
or laughing at a silly joke,
I'm comfortable with you
dear friend.
Miss, Ms., Mrs.
I will soon have been all three.
I practice writing my
soon-to-be new name.
Then I'll have
another new ring
to ring around
my engagement ring.
Oh, ring, ring, ring around ring,
my mind is obsessed
with my new rings!

WEDDING DAY

Our life together begins
on a joyous note
as the wedding march
invites excited guests
to share each beginning
moment
of our new life together.

By giving me away to you,
my parents give witness
to their utter trust
in your ability
to be my loving partner.

We'll enjoy each other for
who we are,
which was the reason
we first fell in love.
Don't try to change me
and I won't try to
change you.

We've grown to love our
independence,
and will now discover
new interdependence
while keeping our own
individuality.

With each other, life will
always be exciting.
May we find
joy and laughter
together
and with our children.

The recessional begins,
rings are exchanged,
God's blessings are on us,
our love declared
and witnessed.

Mr. and Mrs . . .
greet your new families
and old friends.

CLASS REUNION

We come together
to celebrate our past
and renew acquaintances,
every reunion a
new beginning to the
high school ending.

How smart we were
at eighteen or thereabouts.
We were going out
into the world armed with
not much more than
enthusiasm,
yet believing we had
more to give
than to receive.

At five years
some were college graduates,
in the permanent workforce,
or parents.

At ten years we were
budding into our prime
with some long-range visions
in place.

Our twenty-fifth found us
mellowing,
maybe not huge successes
in the material way,
but winners
in many other ways.
Mostly, we're just plain folks.

Other reunions are a bonus.
How's your family,
your health, and all the
other questions grandparents
ask each other?

Yes, my classmates,
my friends from long ago,
tell me about your life
and all the ordinary events
of it while we share
family photos and
brag about what really counts:
family - yours, mine,
and our school family.

Old friends, classmates,
I wish you well.
I wish you happiness
and good health,
and I wish you
many more reunions.

CHILDREN

Looking back in hindsight
I discover how unfair
I was at times,
expecting the firsts
to come sooner and oftener
than they did for
other people's children.

Did I allow you enough time
to be uninhibited,
free in spirit and heart, or
was I too fussy?

When you started school
I watched for signs of genius,
asking myself
how you were different,
rather than
how you were the same.
Did I set
unrealistic goals for you?

Worry was my second name.
I never wanted you
to be touched by life's problems,
so I made them mine

137

and tried to
solve them for you.

But there were many
good times as well;
too many to count.

We laughed together
while playing, working,
and vacationing,
seeing humor in
everyday situations
while enjoying
each other's company.

Somehow you have all
managed to survive
beautifully
with my guidance
and sometimes in spite of it.

You have been an inspiration,
a joy, and the reason that
gives purpose to my life.
I needed to
tell you that, and
I needed to say,
"Thank you!"

So . . . Who Gave You Birth?

You'd do that
to me?
So . . . who
gave you birth?
My waist
was eighteen inches . . .
a size eight,
no less.

Men turned
and looked twice
when I
came in a room.
I was the
envy of women
and the
pride of my family . . .
a star figure.

So . . . now I'm
a little rotund.
So . . . .my personality
has to shine
a little more.
All of this
I don't mind,
as long as
my child
loves me more
than life itself.
So . . . I say again,
who gave you birth?
I could have been
a
   movie
      star.

LITTLE BROTHER

What a nuisance you were
little brother,
always tagging along
or tattling on me.
You always knew
how to push
mom's buttons
to get me
in trouble.

Thank goodness
you finally started school
and began making friends
of your own.

Now you had someone else
to keep you busy
and out of my hair.

When love finally came
into your life
you quit
spying on me
at last
and began avoiding me
with much enthusiasm
as you used
in your previous
pursuit.

When true love
finally hit
the two of us,
a new you
began to emerge.

You became
a different person,
one who is now
a lot of fun
to be with.

And to think
the new you
was hidden
and surfaced
only when you
became an adult.
Or did it?

BIG BROTHER

I know you
always thought of me
as a nuisance,
and I guess I was,
but it was only
because I wanted to be
just like you,
and the only way
I could do that
was to follow you around
and imitate
everything you did.

When girls
came into your life
my favorite pastime
was unashamedly
spying on you
out of curiosity
and just plain
mischief.

Now that we're
both adults
and have mates
of our own,
a lot has changed.
Rather than
avoid each other,
it's wonderful
to be together
and watch our families
cavort as only
relatives can.

Times change,
but some things don't.
You'll always be
my big brother
and I'll always
look up to you,
but now we're friends.
I like it that way.

LITTLE SISTER

Little sister,
I have to tell you,
you absolutely
drove me nuts
when we were kids.
You were always
snooping in my closet,
eyeing which dresses
would be yours shortly,
and setting your sights
on the next
skirt or sweater
that would switch over
from my closet to yours.

Every morning
when I put
the finishing touches
on my makeup,
there you were,
watching every
move I made,
later imitating
what you saw.

When I married,
it suddenly
struck me
that the little pest
wouldn't be there
each morning
watching me get ready
for my day
or later snooping
through my closet.

And then it hit me
like a bolt of lightning:
my life as I
always knew it
would never be again.
I was not an
intricate part of
my family anymore,
but had to begin one
of my own.
And then the tears came
and I wished I could
tell you I always loved you.

Big Sister

My dream was always
to grow big enough
to fit into
your wonderful clothes.
Hand-me-downs
never bothered me
as long as
they were yours,
but nothing ever
looked as good
or felt as comfortable
on me
as it did on you.

149

Every day I'd watch you
comb your beautiful hair
and put the finishing touches
on your makeup.
Teachers always compared us,
but I was so proud of you
it pleased me
when they saw similarities.

You married when
I was very young
so I missed out
on all the fun
of learning girl stuff
from you.

Although I was
a tag along always,
and therefore a pest
to be ignored,
I realized your marriage
was the beginning
of the end
to our family life
as we knew it.

We would never
be the same.

I was afraid
to say it
while we were
growing up
for fear you'd laugh,
but please know always
that I'm so proud of you.

GIFTS TO MY CHILDREN

If I had
three gifts
to give my children,
what would
my choices be?

The first one
leaves no doubt;
I would hope
my children
know how deeply
they are loved,
and how loveable
they are.

Second, I choose justice,
and am quite sure
my children
think of me as just,
because I embarrass them
quite regularly
as is the
prerogative of justice.

Third, have they
learned to look at life
through eyes of humor?
Life's lessons often
come hard and fast,
but tempered with humor
and good spirit,
nothing can get
the best of us.

These are my gifts:
unconditional love,
justice as its own reward,
and humor enough
to never take oneself
too seriously.
Love, justice, and humor,
if you've enjoyed them,
pass them on, please.

TRADITION

Tradition is
a quiet presence
in each life.
It may be
associated with
a holiday,
time of the year,
or feeling of a moment.

Children quite often
begin a tradition based on
a previous happy memory
they want to replay,
so they call it
tradition.

155

Oldtimers remember
the smells and tastes
of their youth,
or feelings of
a fleeting moment.

Tradition is
most always happy,
because who wants to relive
a bad memory?

Tradition is longstanding
or brand new,
depending on how
the fancy hits us.

One person's tradition
is not another's.
One person's joy
may be another's sorrow.

Be what may,
tradition is
a quiet presence
in each life.

Family Reunion

We gather in anticipation,
joy unbridled,
to renew the love
and closeness
of our youth.

We are family together,
with all our
defenses down
and failures exposed,
to share
and be nurtured
with unconditional
love.

Success embraces some
while eluding others.
Cousins cavort
while newer spouses,
meeting again,
become further absorbed
into family history.
Siblings revert
to behavior of their youth,
and laughter
comes easily.

SPARE US!

Why is it
grownup kids
get such a kick
out of shocking parents
with long past
tales of terror
never known
to mom and dad
as children grew?

Stuffing beds
when they snuck out,
silently rolling the family car
down quiet, unlit streets,
'til halfway down the block,
skipping school,
then playing hooky
at their favorite beach,
reclining on sun drenched sand
while reading the latest novels,
are only some of the
"shocking" tales
children share with parents
in our maturing years.

Kids drank at parties
before they came of age,
smoked cigarettes or worse
while running free with
their howling pack
of teenage hormones,
refusing to be tamed.

Please spare us from
such unrequested knowledge!
Let us live in innocence
now that the worst
is obviously
behind us.
Do you really think
your parents
were as stupid
as you paint them?

Maybe so,
or maybe no,
or maybe
we just choose
to keep our little secrets
and wallow in sweet innocence,
so spare us!

HALLOWEEN

The witching hour
comes tonight
and with it three foot
ghosts and goblins
clutching bags of treats
to make the dentist
beat his breast
and beg for mercy
for his tiny patients.

Anticipation
for the hallowed evening
consumes two months
of waking hours
as future spooks
decide who or what
they'll be,
fledgling actors all,
anticipating their evening

when the curtain
finally rises
and they say their
three word line:
Trick or Treat.

So have a wonderful
opening
and closing night.
And when
the final curtain
comes down,
I hope the anticipation,
dreams, and curtain call
were as fun
as you imagined
they would be.
Happy Halloween!

CHILDREN AND THE OCEAN

Giggling children
run into the ocean
to greet
an approaching wave.

Giggles grow
to belly laughs
as children
change direction
and rush to shore
outscurrying
the foaming water.

Sometimes
the gigglers
decide to
ride waves
ashore,
then scurry
from the undertow.

Waves roll in,
undertow pulls out,
while giggles
fill the air.

A GRANDMA AGAIN

So you're a grandma
for the second time
while I'm waiting
for number one!
Seems a wee bit
masochistic.
(I should have been
a nun.)

I hold
everybody's babies
hoping luck will
come my way.
Can you imagine
how downright boring I'll be
when it finally is
my day?

I'll call everyone
to tell them
(even people
I don't know,)
that I'm gonna
be a grandma.

"Hot dog!
It's finally so!"

But until
that day arrives,
I'll vicariously dream.
"Congratulations!
Hugs and kisses!"
(I think I'm gonna scream.)

NEW GRANDMA

I'm a grandma!
Yes, I am!
Wonder of wonders
has happened to me
and the joy
in my heart
is taking over
and flying me as high
as a soaring bird.

My own dear grandchild;
what fun we're
going to have.

I will renew my wonder
of nature's beauty
all over again
through your eyes,
being teacher and student
at the same time.

I've learned patience
throughout my years
of motherhood,
and the wisdom
to be a good listener so I
can learn from you.

Your birth
rejuvenates the earth
and renews the promise
of God's presence
with us always.
Did you know
that every hair
of your head is counted,
even the ones
yet to be?

So hold on to your bonnet
my dear little one.
You and Grandma
will be having
fun, fun, fun!

GRANDMOTHER

The job of motherhood
is a paradox,
being both long and hard,
yet short and enjoyable
at the same time.
I learned to juggle
listening and speaking,
trying to use wisdom
in deciding when to do each.

As years passed
and my children
grew in independence,
I had time for some
independence of my own.

And now the bonus:
grandchildren.

I wish I 'd been
as relaxed and patient
with your parent
as I am with you,
my grandchild,
when rocking you on my lap,
reading or listening.
(Why did it take me so long
to become a good listener?)

God help me resist
preaching to you
about the good old days,
standing in judgement,
or giving advice.

You and I will
share your childhood
and my golden years,
always learning
from each other.
And when my time here is up,
I hope you're left
with memories of
happy days we had together.

YOU HAVE A KNACK

There's something
very special
about you.
You have a knack
for saying the
very best thing
at the absolute
right time,
and even better,
for saying
absolutely nothing
at the very best times.

We can
be with each other
and communicate
perfectly
in complete silence.
I like that.
I'm comfortable
with you.

Sometimes,
my days are so long
they run into night.
You never tell me
it's too late
to call.
You make me feel
like the excitement
of hearing my voice
has completed
your happy day,
when I know
the reverse
is probably true.

Yes, my special friend,
you have the knack . . .
of bringing sunshine
into each room
you enter.
May you, too,
be blessed
with a friend
just like yourself.
I hope it's me.
I try to be.

I Remember My Dear Best Friend

Playing house
and other games,
climbing trees
and reading
in our favorite tree,
sleeping out in our jungle hammocks,
stealing apples,
soaping windows on Halloween,
spending holidays together,
joining neighborhood games,
going to Saturday movie matinees,
running errands,
swiping homemade cookies,
ditching her cousin,
taking care of her baby brother
when we were 12,
writing and illustrating a story,
playing "Sally and Jane,"
training our dogs,
being world famous photographers,
sucking nectar from lilacs,
working in the yard,
selling lemonade,
sitting on chairs by the curb
and counting cars

that waved to us,
double dating,
riding in a rumble seat,
pledging the same high school sorority,
and having so many other wonderful times
together.
My dear best friend,
how we loved each other.

FRIEND OF MY YOUTH

My friend of so many years,
what were your
first memories
of our friendship?
Did you remember
beginning grade school
together after that
first summer
of peeking at each other
from behind
our backyard bushes?

We progressed
to hiding behind
the birdbath
so we could
better examine each other.

It wasn't long
before we were inseparable.
I could hardly wait
to gulp down breakfast
and run next door,
calling for you
to begin our day together,
not wanting to waste
any of it.

We pretended,
we played dress-up
and house,
and board games
until arguments
broke up our fun.

We were closer than sisters
and shared secrets
no one else
would be privy to ever.
Double dating in high school
continued our
fun and closeness.
Later we each
married and moved away,
but our paths
crossed again.

Only this time
you were critically ill.
We could each see
the end of our
worldly friendship in sight.
You suffered so,
but were so brave.

Now you have
one more duty, dear friend.
Will you please put in
a good word for me,
and save me a seat
next to you?

181

WOMAN TO WOMAN

Woman to woman
it's fun to talk,
while we visit over coffee,
or go for a walk.
How's your family doing,
pets and the job?
Are you happy in general
or does your freedom feel robbed?

We listen and counsel,
suggest or not,
then try to keep cool
when we really feel hot.
Many days we feel like
we're losing our minds,
as we labor continually
at our daily grind.

We juggle so many
jobs each day,
some free at home,
others for pay.
We labor for family

out of love and tradition;
we work for ourselves
to better our condition.

But I do need to know,
when all chips are down,
and I feel the world
looking at me like a clown.
I need to know then,
you are there in the wings,
my dear friend,
nonjudgmentally
telling me things.

Like what a
good friend
I've been,
loyal and true,
and how I have
helped you
whenever you're blue.
Yes, woman to woman
it's fun to talk,
as we visit over coffee
or go for a walk.

What Goes Around

What goes around
comes around;
I know I'm
getting older.
My mother
said these words
to me;
I never
understood them.

Now I understand.

Kindness placed
upon life's table
revolves right
back to us.
Time spent
with children
pays rewards
as we see them
enter adulthood
with values written
in their hearts.

What goes around
comes around,
no matter
good or bad.
We speak of
heavenly justice;
I wonder if
it's now?

Whether I give myself
or worldly goods
I get much more
in return,
like love, or peace,
or justice,
coming back
a hundredfold.

Life is good.
My circular table
keeps rotating
day by day.
I must take care!
What's put upon it,
comes back
in different ways.

CRUEL WORDS

How easily those
cutting words
slip out an
unthinking mouth,
venting anger of the speaker
in a matter
of seconds,
but remembered
by the receiver
forever.

Better it would be
to close the mouth
and choke those
disrespectful,
hurting words,
never allowing them
to be heard by any
but in the mind
of the speaker.

Life passes all too quickly.
Kind words
never have
enough time
to be said.
Often, death catches us
too soon,
trapping unsaid
loving words
in hearts,
never to be spoken,
while cruel ones
slip out,
never to be retrieved.

Kind words leave
a joyful memory;
cruel words
nullify them
forever.

Too Busy

I call my friend
to see how life
is treating her today,
and find out
we need a date
to talk together
on the phone,
but can never
meet anywhere
for lunch . . . .
Too Busy.

When looking for
some hardy souls
to help at church
or school
or other jobs,
regulars will always hear
about prospects'
busy schedules,
making everyone. . .
Too Busy.

Children needing
companionship
or extra hugs

come to parents
anticipating conversation,
but leave dejected
because parents are,
right now,
and in the
days to come . . .
Too Busy.

I learn a lesson
hearing people talk about
exciting, busy lives.
I know I'll never be
too busy for my friends
or those in need,
listening always
to my children
and my mate,
and no matter
how my days are filled
I'll try never to retort . . .
Too Busy.

Women Need Women

Women need each other.
A woman's best friend
is usually another woman.
Family is wonderful,
husbands are wonderful,
but every woman
needs other women to talk with
about her own interests.

Kids will be kids, and oh yes,
husbands will be husbands.
Women experience the same
frustrations with each.

At times a mother feels
like everyone's servant
with no identity of her own.
Occasionally, her husband may be
a bit insensitive,
self-centered, or autocratic,
causing her to feel like
chucking it all.

But sometimes women can
make it right
by talking, comforting,
encouraging,
and reassuring each other.
Together, women can
laugh at problems, thus
saving a few marriages
and healing a few wounds.
They're generally
good friends to each other
whether talking seriously
or speaking with a
sense of humor.

Adjusting to marriage,
having a family, raising children,
doing housework, and working
at church and school
are activities
women share in common.
Unfortunately, what's important
to women isn't always
of interest to their families,
which is why women
need each other.

FULL CIRCLE

When I was
a young woman
I remember
my father
talking about death.
I didn't want
to hear about it;
my father
was going to
live forever.
He said,
"I remember
my friends
losing their grandparents,
next it was
my friends' parents . . .
now, it's us."

Then I
lost my grandparents.
But mixed in
with their loss,
my younger brother
died;
that wasn't
supposed to be.
Next my father
died,
tending his flowers
in the garden.
Then my mother.

Pretty soon
I'll be a grandparent,
and when it's my turn,
I'll have come full circle.

THE CHILD IN ME

Although I'm a parent
with adult responsibility
and commitment to a job,
the child in me
sometimes surfaces
and demands attention.

On hot days
when I see a sprinkler
watering a thirsty lawn,
I want to toss
clothes and cares
to the wind
and run through
the cold invigorating spray
with no inhibitions.

I need to shed
responsibility
occasionally
and leave
the worry of survival
to someone else.

And when I'm ill,
or lonely,
or depressed,
I want to run into arms
that mean protection
and say,
"take care of me,"
or simply
have a good friend
with whom I can share
the child in me.

COMING HOME

So many years
have passed
since our family
left my childhood home.
They've been
years of wandering,
many spent
trying to find
the real person
who finally emerged
after years of
nurturing and growth.

Travels have taken me
on so many
paths of adventure
and discovery,
some exciting,
some terrifying,
some sad beyond words.

Now, for a short time,
I return to the
place of my birth
and home of my youth.

Memories mix
with emotions,
and floodgates
of decades
open reluctantly,
releasing all the
good and bad
cornerstones of
who I am.
I can't go back,
but I can
understand the present
a little better.
I am who I am.

CHANGING ROLES

Not long ago I held you
in my arms
to feed you,
my dear, helpless child.

As a parent
I was nursemaid,
teacher, comforter,
and quite simply,
all things to you.

As you grew,
your funny ways entertained
and delighted everyone.
You loved being
the center of attention.
We nurtured your
inborn self-confidence
lovingly,
even when you
entered those frightening
teen years
and were lost temporarily
in self-doubt.

But this, too, passed,
and a metamorphosis
happened to me.

Instead of being
mostly a caregiver,
I also became
your companion and friend.
It was fun
going to lunch together
and talking about
meaningful adult interests.

Then you married
and we shared other secrets.
When grandchildren
were born
a wonderful new world
became mine.

How quickly
wisdom of maturity
slipped away,
leaving me less confident
and more fearful
of so many things.

My child now feeds me
and holds me in loving arms.
My life is full circle.

GREETING CARDS AVAILABLE

OF YOUR FAVORITE POEMS

MINIMUM ORDER: 12 CARDS

$1.50 per 5X7 Frameable card & envelope
PLUS $3.00 postage and handling

TITLES _____

_____

_____

_____

_____

YOUR NAME _____

ADDRESS _____

_____

_____

_____

PHONE (_____) _____

SEND TO: **ST. JOHN'S PUBLISHING**
6824 OAKLAWN AVENUE
EDINA, MINNESOTA 55435

FOR DISCOUNTS/MORE INFORMATION, CALL:
(612) 920-9044 OR
FAX (612) 920-7662

GREETING CARDS AVAILABLE
OF YOUR FAVORITE POEMS

MINIMUM ORDER: 12 CARDS

$1.50 per 5X7 Frameable card, envelope
PLUS $3.00 postage and handling

TITLES _____

_____

_____

_____

_____

YOUR NAME _____

ADDRESS _____

_____

_____

_____

PHONE (_____) _____

SEND TO: **ST. JOHN'S PUBLISHING**
6824 OAKLAWN AVENUE
EDINA, MINNESOTA 55435

FOR DISCOUNTS/MORE INFORMATION, CALL:
(612) 920-9044 OR
FAX (612) 920-7662

ST. JOHN'S PUBLISHING

6824 OAKLAWN AVENUE
EDINA, MINNESOTA 55435

Please send me _____ copy/copies of **Love, Life & Chocolate Chip Cookies** (ISBN 0-938577-10-7). I am enclosing $6.95 plus $1.50 for shipping per copy.

Please send me _____ copy/copies of **Surviving Motherhood** (ISBN 0-938577-00-X). I am enclosing $6.95 plus $1.50 for shipping per copy.

Please send me _____ copy/copies of **Parenting a Business** (ISBN 0-938577-04-2). I am enclosing $14.95 plus $1.50 for shipping per copy.

Please send me _____ copy/copies of **Kids + Modeling = Money** (ISBN 0-13-515172-4). I am enclosing $9.95 (hardcover) plus $1.50 for shipping per copy.

NAME _____

ADDRESS _____

_____

_____

_____

_____

ST. JOHN'S PUBLISHING

6824 OAKLAWN AVENUE
EDINA, MINNESOTA 55435

Please send me _____ copy/copies of **Love, Life & Chocolate Chip Cookies** (ISBN 0-938577-10-7). I am enclosing $6.95 plus $1.50 for shipping per copy.

Please send me _____ copy/copies of **Surviving Motherhood** (ISBN 0-938577-00-X). I am enclosing $6.95 plus $1.50 for shipping per copy.

Please send me _____ copy/copies of **Parenting a Business** (ISBN 0-938577-04-2). I am enclosing $14.95 plus $1.50 for shipping per copy.

Please send me _____ copy/copies of **Kids + Modeling = Money** (ISBN 0-13-515172-4). I am enclosing $9.95 (hardcover) plus $1.50 for shipping per copy.

NAME _____

ADDRESS _____

_____

_____

_____

_____